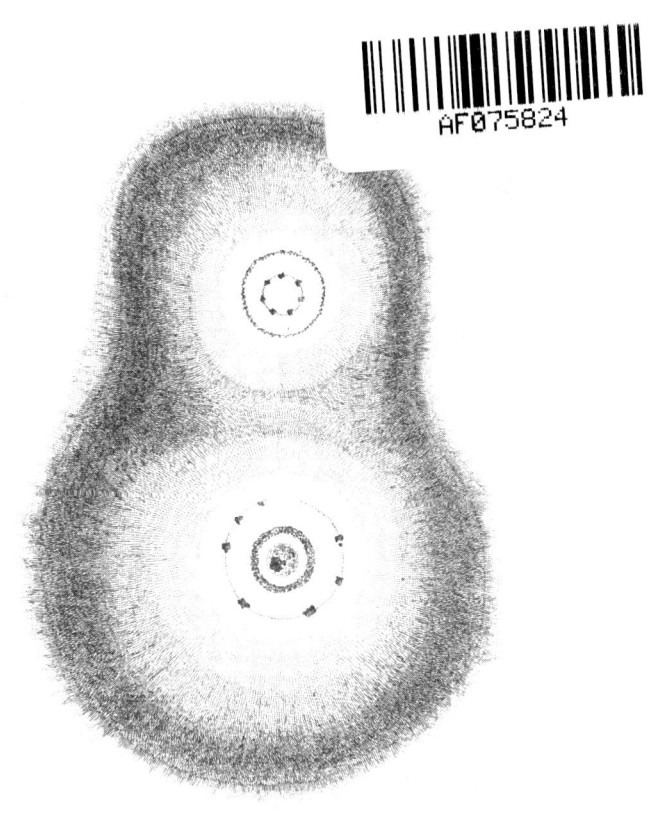

ABOVE: *Plan of ancient monuments on Killin Hill co. Louth*

First published 2024
This edition © Hector McDonnell 2024

Published by Wooden Books Ltd.
Glastonbury, Somerset.
www.woodenbooks.com

British Library Cataloguing in Publication Data
McDonnell, H.
Megalithic Ireland

A CIP catalogue record for this book
may be obtained from the British Library.

ISBN-10: 1-907155-65-1
ISBN-13: 978-1-907155-65-9

All rights reserved.
For permission to reproduce any part of this
megalithic marvel please contact the publishers.

Designed and typeset in Glastonbury, UK.
Printed in India on FSC® certified papers by
Quarterfold Printabilities Pvt. Ltd.

MEGALITHIC IRELAND

CAIRNS, TOMBS, HENGES & CIRCLES

Giant's Grave, co. Sligo. W. F Wakeman.

Hector McDonnell

To Wendy and Rose, with all my love.

CONTENTS

Introduction	1
Carrowmore	2
The Kissing Stone	4
Passage Tombs: Carrowkeel	6
Court Cairns	8
Magheraganrush	10
Creevykeel & Clontygora	12
More Court Cairns	14
Portal Tombs	16
Labby Rock & Brownshill	18
Poulnabrone & Kilclooney	20
Linkardstown Cists	22
The Loughcrew Complex	24
The Boyne Valley Complex: Dowth	26
Newgrange	28
Knowth	30
The Hill of Tara	32
Henges	34
Grange & Ballynoe	36
More Stone Circles	38
Recumbent Stone Circles	40
Wedge Tombs	42
Labbacalle Wedge Tomb	44
Stone Rows	46
Standing Stones	48
More Standing Stones	50
Mystical Memories	52
Stone Magic	54
Ireland's Main Megalithic Sites	56

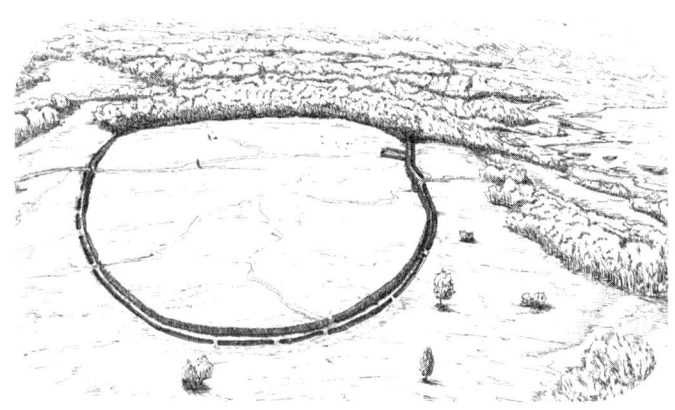

ABOVE: c.4150BC Neolithic causewayed enclosure at Magheraboy (by John Murphy).
BELOW: Complex at the confluence of two rivers, Balregan, Dundalk, co. Louth.

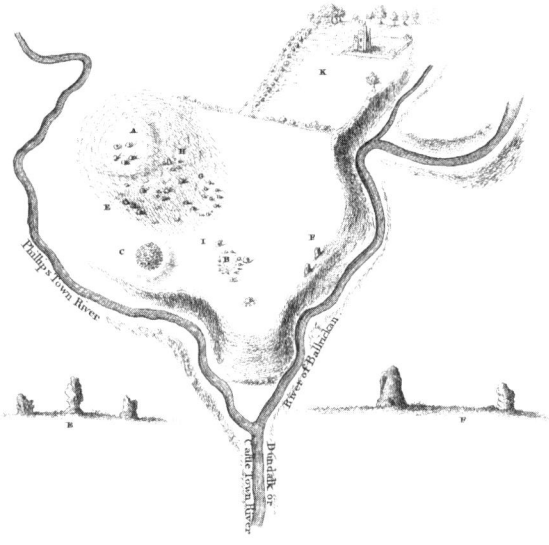

INTRODUCTION

The creation of large scale landscape monuments was integral the Neolithic communities that first arose in the Near East more than 12,000 years ago. As these peoples dispersed and resettled they brought their surveying, stone working, farming and pottery skills with them. By the 5th millennium bc, some had reached Central Europe, where they built large 'rondels', often oriented towards midsummer sunrises and sunsets, while others moved westwards by boat, creating megalithic monuments, often with solar or lunar alignments, all the way to Armorica (Brittany).

A few centuries later, some Neolithic people (who typically had black hair and blue eyes) reached the Irish south coast. This is indicated by a few cattle bones, a sheep's tooth and some pottery fragments dating from c.4350 BC. Around c.4150 BC they created the oldest causewayed enclosure in the British Isles, at Magheraboy in Sligo (*Machaire Buí*, 'Yellow Plain', opposite top), with timber posts about 1.5m high. They also started building modest megalithic monuments with capstones balanced on upright stones (orthostats). One, at Killaclohane (*Coill an Chlocháin*, 'the wood of the stone structure') in co. Kerry, dated to c.3800 BC, contained the remains of two people, some pottery sherds, flint arrowheads and a javelin head.

Meanwhile, a somewhat different form of the Neolithic tradition spread across Britain and crossed into the North of Ireland from Scotland c.4000 BC, raising its own type of megalithic shrine in the areas it settled, changing the Irish landscape forever.

This little book tells the story of megalithic Ireland through its extraordinary and enduring ancient monuments.

CARROWMORE
a complex cemetery

Around 3750 BC the settlers from the south began creating a large megalithic cemetery at Carrowmore (*Ceathrú Mór*, 'Big Quarterland') co. Sligo. The site remained in use until c.3000 BC.

Thirty tombs survive. Each once consisted of a central pentagonal dolmen chamber standing on a low clay and stone platform edged by boulder circles (sometimes two) of 30 to 40 stones, with more stones lining the entrances. At the centre of the whole complex is Listoghil (*Lios a' tSeagail*, 'Rye Court'), a huge cairn surrounding a dolmen, with an open passageway pointing to where the sun rises over Ballygawley Mountain at Samhain and Imbolc. A great fire was burnt on this ground before it was built, probably after the removal of an earlier tomb, for the bones here are c.3500 BC, while the surrounding dolmens are several centuries older. The other tombs are all arranged around Listoghil, and all have their entrances aligned toward it. Two important sites nearby are Knocknarea's cairn in which the goddess-queen Maeve is said to stand, a weapon in each hand, and the rock rings at Clover Hill (*below, by Margaret Stokes*).

ABOVE: Carrowmore Circles 56 and 57, by William Wakeman, 1879.

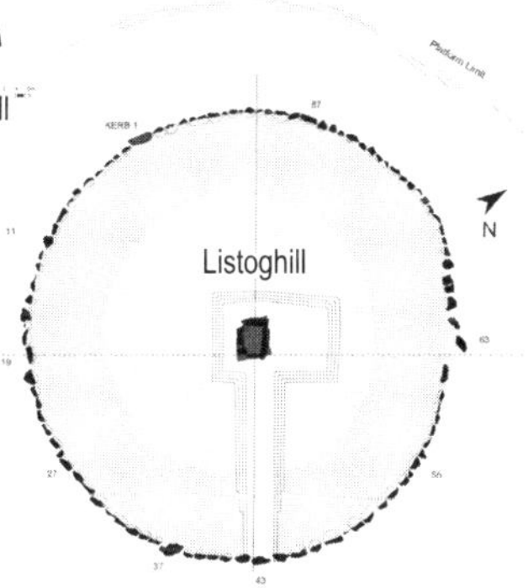

LEFT: George Petrie's draft map of Carrowmore, 1837. ABOVE: View of Listoghill, the centre of the Carrowmore complex. SURVEY: Pádraig Meehan.

The Kissing Stone
and other Carrowmore sites

The Kissing Stone (*Leaba na Fían*, 'Warriors' Bed') is the best preserved Carrowmore dolmen. It is surrounded by a 37ft diameter circle of 32 stones (*see illustration below, based on a original by Gabriel Beranger, 1779*). The capstone balances on the points of three stones, and its entrance looks at the equinox sunrise over Carns Hill. Its excavators in 1977 and 1978 found:

> *80 small fragments of bone, greyish-white in colour, possibly calcined. Along with these were the tooth of a young pig, a mussel shell and a cockle shell, two small helix shells, several portions of other shells, and a fine 'thumb-flint' or 'strike-a-light'.*

There were also fragments of pins, an arrowhead and a small limestone ball, while about two hundred unopened seashells lay in a pit outside the boulder circle.

ABOVE: Circle 22, Carrowmore, watercolour by William Wakeman, 1879.

ABOVE: Dolmen 4, Carrowmore, Wakeman, 1879.

ABOVE: West Cairn, Carns Hill, Wakeman, 1879

ABOVE: Dolmen 37, Carrowmore, Wakeman, 1879

ABOVE: The Barnasrahy pot.

CARROWKEEL PASSAGE TOMBS
aligned to the sun

In the fourth millennium BC new structures began to appear, with corbelled stone passages leading to chambers, covered with large cairns. Many of these 'passage tombs' were carefully designed so rays of sunlight entered them at significant moments during the ritual year, for example, the solstices or equinoxes. Large stones and smaller quartz rocks ('sun stones') were hauled and sited across the landscape. At Carrowkeel, co. Sligo, 14 passage tombs, mostly of the classic cruciform shape, were constructed of limestone from c.3500 BC.

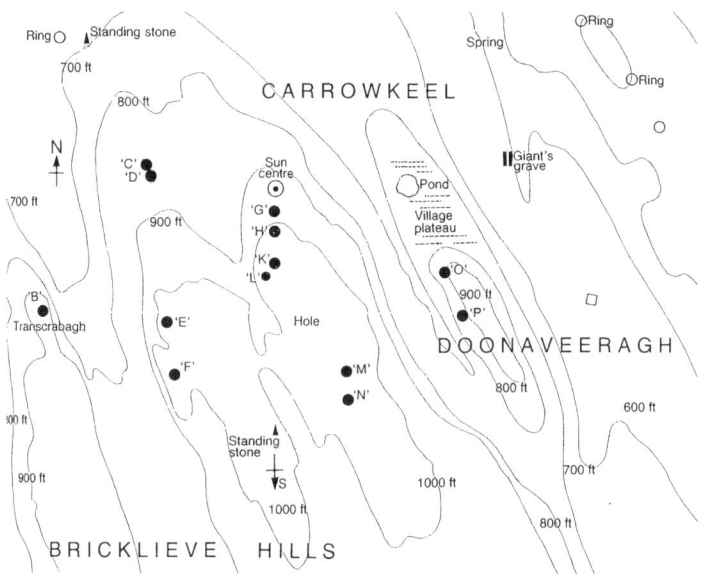

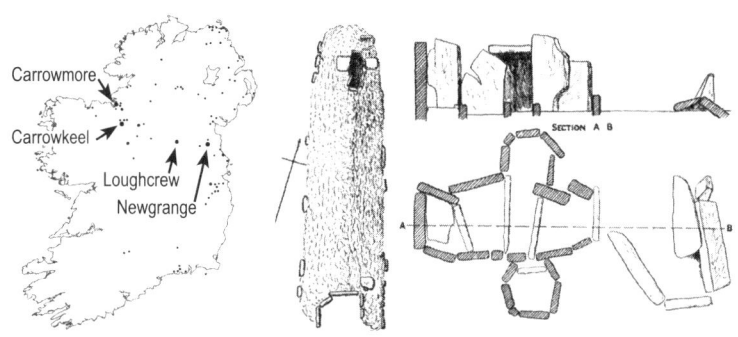

ABOVE LEFT: Distribution of Irish Passage Tombs. RIGHT: **CARROWKEEL E. CAIRN E**'s passage is aligned towards summer solstice sunset/winter solstice sunrises over Knocknarea hill. The full moon enters the chamber every 18.6 years.

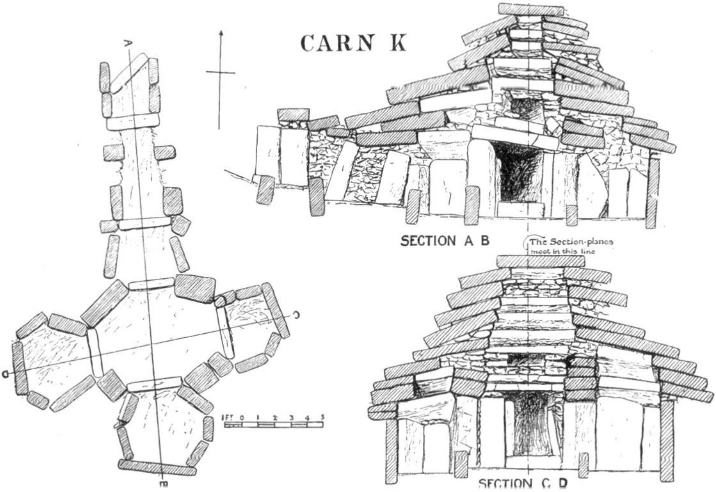

FACING PAGE: The Carrowkeel complex, co. Sligo (Ceathrú Caol, 'Narrow Quarterland'), on Bricklieve Mountain, c. 3500 - c. 2500 BC. Built by neolithic cattle-farmers from Brittany. The complex contains 14 passage graves. ABOVE: Carrowkeel K, by Macalister & Prager, 1911.

COURT CAIRNS
in the north

The Irish settlers from Scotland built different monuments from their southern neighbours. Between c.3900 and 3500 BC more than 390 "court cairns" were erected north of a line from Dublin to Galway.

These structures have an entrance on to an open courtyard which is connected to one or more covered burial galleries and chambers. Ashes from cremation pyres have been found, and human remains intermingled with worked flints, axes, stone beads, bone and antler pins, seashells, animal bones and broken pottery. During this period, quartz was much in demand, its translucence and the flash of light emitted when struck gave rise to its Irish name, *grianchloch*, 'sun stone'.

Circa 2500 to 2000 BC, a series of disruptions, including a large volcanic eruption in Iceland, caused a decade of minimal sunlight, during which the bubonic plague also appeared. Population numbers fell, and court cairns were largely abandoned by new settlers.

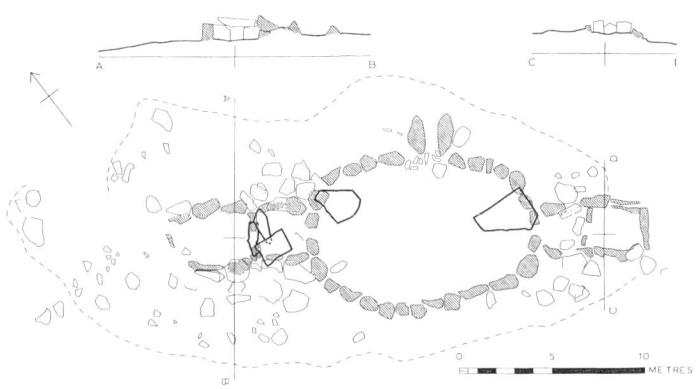

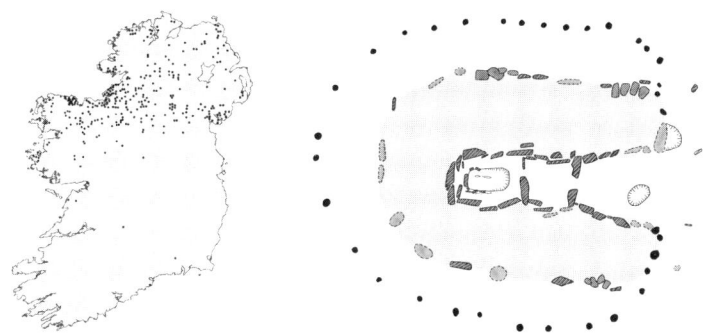

ABOVE LEFT: Distribution of Court Cairns. RIGHT: Plan of **SHANBALLYEDMUND**, co. Tipperary (Seanbhaile Éamainn, 'Éamann's old townland'), one of only two court tombs in Munster and South Leinster. Its U-shaped court (4 × 3m) leads to a gallery with two chambers. 34 post holes about 2m from the kerb, indicate that a wooden structure surrounded the tomb. The bones of six people were found in 1958, along with flint arrow heads and Neolithic pottery.

ABOVE: Artist's impression of a court tomb. FACING PAGE: Plan of **BALLYGLASS I**, co. Mayo, (Baile Glas, 'Grey Townland'), one of a group of thirty around Bunatrahir Bay. The court measures 11.50 m x 7.25 m, its orthostats are all in place, as are some kerb stones, corbels and a sandstone lintel. The tomb was partly built over an Early Neolithic rectangular timber house. Radio carbon dating of 2320 BC, indicates its last use.

MAGHERAGHANRUSH
and Rathlacken and Creggandevesky

MAGHERAGHANRUSH COURT TOMB, Deerpark, co. Sligo, (*Machaire Chon Rois*, 'the Plain of Ros's Hound') was built c.3000 BC (*illustrated below and opposite*). Its initial 'U' shape was later increased in size and turned into an oval court, 30m long, consisting of a gallery with two chambers at one end and a single chamber at the other. Some lintels are still in place, giving it the name "the Irish Stonehenge". Both animal and human bones have been found.

RATHLACKEN, co. Mayo, (*Ráth Leacáin* 'Fort of Stone Slabs') is well preserved (*not shown*). It has three chambers and a circular court. Cremation deposits were found in one chamber with early Neolithic pottery and stone implements. It was still in use c.2000 BC.

CREGGANDEVESKY, co. Tyrone, (*Creagán Duibh Uisce*, 'Stony Place of Black Water') is dated to c.3500 BC. Its gallery entrance has a massive lintel. It is one of two court cairns oriented towards midwinter sunrise.

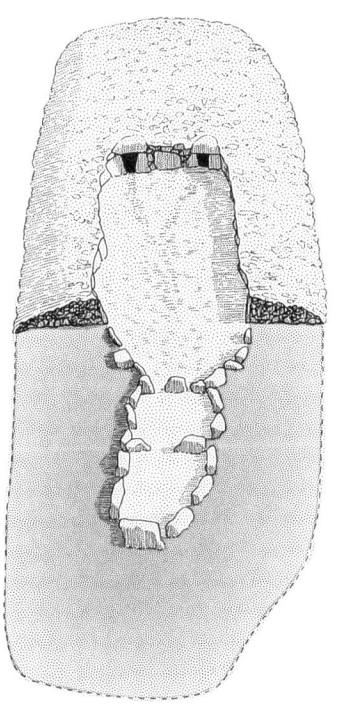

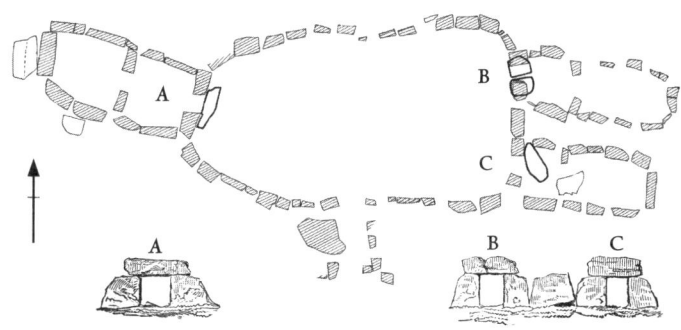

ABOVE: Plan of the large Magheraghanrush court cairn, co. Sligo, showing the locations of the remaining lintels. BELOW: W.F Wakeman's watercolour of the site, painted in 1879. FACING PAGE: The same site again, as drawn by Frazer William in 1905. It is also known as the Giant's Grave, or the Druid's Altar.

CREEVYKEEL & CLONTYGORA
two wedge-shaped court cairns

CREEVYKEEL, co. Sligo, (*Chraobhach Caol*, 'Narrow Thicket') is an unusually large monument with a wedge-shaped cairn. A narrow passage at its eastern end leads into the 15 × 9m oval inner court. Its orthostats are of local sandstone studded with quartz. The gallery's two chambers are aligned so the equinox rising sun lights up its backstone. Three small chambers were added to the western end of the cairn. Its earliest phase is dated to c.3500 BC.

CLONTYGORA, co. Armagh (*Cluainte gabhra*, 'Goats' Meadows'). Known locally as the 'King's Ring' this court tomb is in a prominent position and very impressive. An imposing façade of orthostats, some over 2.7m tall, lines the U-shaped court. Unusually, it looks north, towards a stream.

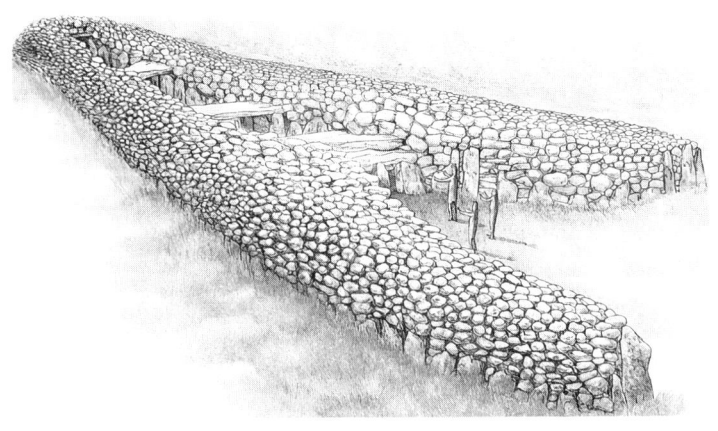

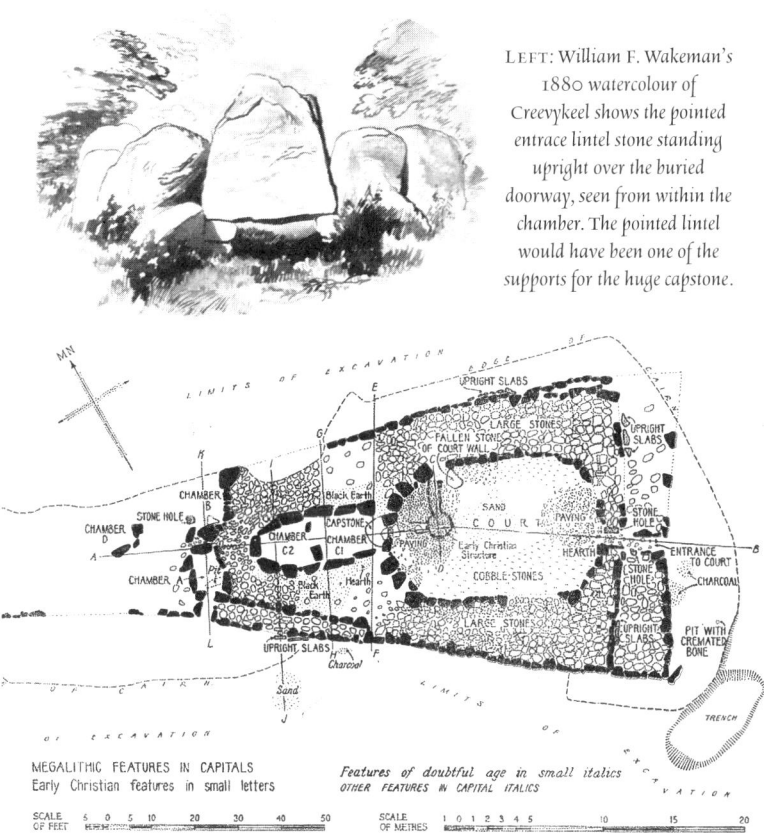

LEFT: William F. Wakeman's 1880 watercolour of Creevykeel shows the pointed entrace lintel stone standing upright over the buried doorway, seen from within the chamber. The pointed lintel would have been one of the supports for the huge capstone.

ABOVE: Hencken's 1935 excavation plan of CREEVYKEEL. During the excavation, the cremated remains of four people were found, along with Neolithic pottery, polished stone axes, flint knives and scrapers and two clay balls. FACING PAGE: Artist's impression of CLONTYGORA court cairn. The gallery entrance has two massive portal stones and the surviving roof slabs and capstone for the first of its three chambers are supported on split granite boulders.

More Court Cairns
a handful from the hundreds

ANTYNANUM, co. Antrim (*An Tigh nAnam* 'The House of Souls') is possibly the longest court cairn in Ireland (*not illustrated*). Its tapering cairn of boulders is up to 2m high and 70m long and two chambers of its gallery can be seen behind the forecourt. The court is formed by fourteen upright slabs and one fallen one. One has a cup-mark on it, and on the north side is a wrecked portal-tomb with a sill stone, and a massive capstone, still sitting on one orthostat.

BALLYMACALDRACK (Dooey's Cairn), co. Antrim (*Baile Mhic Ualdraig*, 'MacAldrack's Townland') has a U-shaped court facing SW (*opposite top*). The gallery's entrance has two portal stones, and two more at its back wall lead into a unique 6m long "cremation passage", dated at c.3800 BC. Three pits sunk into its cobbled floor held the cremated bones of 5-6 adults packed in around three posts which probably supported an 'excarnation platform' where bodies were defleshed by birds.

ANNAGHMARE, co. Armagh (*Áth na Marbh*, 'Ford of the Dead') has two portal stones marking the entrance to the 7m long gallery; its three chambers are divided by pairs of jamb stones (*lower, opposite*).

COHAW, co. Cavan (Cothabháil 'Sustenance') is the finest Irish double court tomb (*not illustrated*). It was originally two single-court tombs facing north and south, under a rectangular cairn 13.5m wide by 25m long. A fifth chamber joined the galleries together.

FARRANMACBRIDE, Columbkille Glen, co. Donegal (*Fearann Mhic Giolla Bhríde*, McGillbride's land) another grand central court cairn.

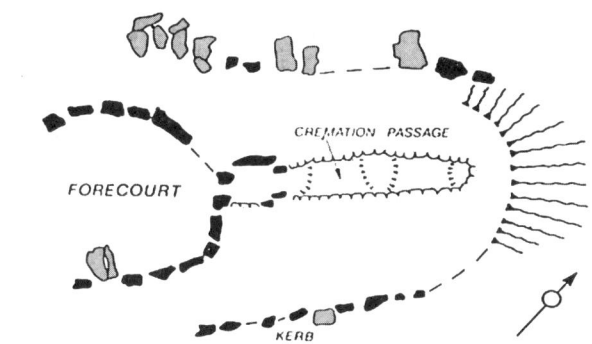

ABOVE: **BALLYMACALDRACK**. A cairn was raised around the early cremation pit, and flagstones laid over the ashes. The court cairn was then built, aligned with the cremation pit, and used from c. 3000 to 2500 BCE, when the court tomb was sealed, its chamber filled with stones, the rubble tapering down into the court, two polished porcellanite axes were left at the entrance.

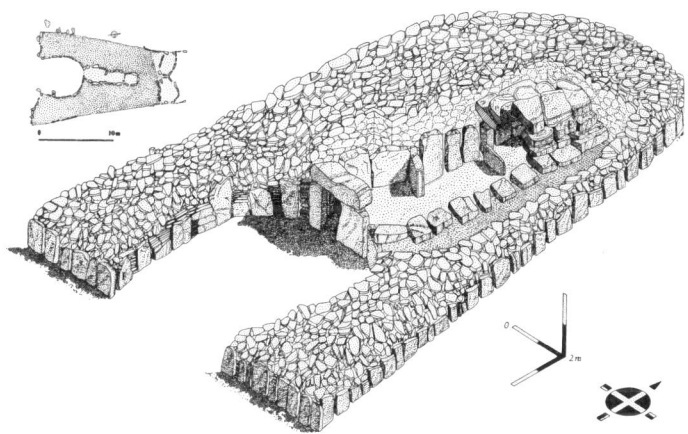

ABOVE: **ANNAGHMARE** is trapezoidal in plan. Two chambers with their own entrances were added at the north end of the cairn when it was increased in size. The kerbs and the court have orthostats with dry-stone walling between them. There is a small standing stone in the forecourt.

Portal tombs
or dolmens or cromlechs

Between 4000 BC and 3000 BC, numerous single-chamber megalithic portal tombs (or dolmens) were constructed, larger versions of the dolmen tradition brought from Armorica. Three or more orthostats support large horizontal capstones, with the heaviest, at Kernanstown in co. Carlow, weighing over a hundred tons. Excavations revealed that the dead in one tomb sat upright against the orthostats until they decomposed, while others were bone repositories.

Some added courts in front of them, or cairns behind them covering burial chambers, and some were aligned towards significant sunrises or sunsets. In the legend of Diarmuit and Gráinne fleeing from Fionn Mac Cumhaill, Diarmuit puts up dolmens for his lover so they can safely sleep in a different place each night.

FAR LEFT: Distribution of Irish portal tombs. LEFT: Corbehagh portal tomb, co. Clare.

CENTRE LEFT: **PROLEEK DOLMEN**, co. Louth (Brú Leac, the 'Bruised Stone') has a 35 ton capstone, and 2m high portal stones. The summer solstice setting sun enters it as it sets over Slieve Gullion. Called the 'Giant's Load', said to be brought by the Scottish giant Para Buidhe Mór Mhac Seoidin who wanted to fight Fionn Mac Cumhaill. He killed a bull and ate it, but then drank water which Fionn had poisoned. He was buried beneath his stone.

BOTTOM LEFT: **HOWTH DOLMEN**, co. Dublin, or Aideen's Grave has a 75 ton quartzite fallen capstone and c.2.5m high portal stones. It is said to be the burial place of Aidín the wife of Oisín's son Oscar, who slew three kings in battle, but was then killed. Aidín died of grief, so Oisín set up this tomb over her remains.

FACING PAGE: Clockwise from top left: Broadstone cromlech, Craigs; Finvoy cromlech, Craigs; Ticloy cromlech; Cloughogan cromlech, Ballygilbert.

LABBY ROCK & BROWNSHILL
some very heavy stones

THE LABBY ROCK (*Leaba*, 'Bed'), or CARRICKGLASS DOLMEN, co. Sligo (*Carraig Glás*, 'Grey Rock') has a massive 70 ton, 5 × 3 × 1.5m capstone of Moytura limestone containing chert and magnesium (*below, by Wakeman*). Bones were found in the chamber in the 19th century.

THIS PAGE: Watercolours by Gabriel Beranger [1725-1817]. ABOVE: Cromlech on the south side of Kilternan hill. BELOW: a. Cromlech at Brenanstown; b. Cromlech at Harold's Town, co. Carlow; c. Cromlech near Rosstrevor, co. Down; d. Mount Venus, co. Dublin.
FACING PAGE: LEFT. Cromlech at Howth co. Dublin; RIGHT. **BROWNSHILL DOLMEN** (Dolmain Chnoic an Bhrúnaigh), co. Carlow, 150 ton granite capstone, the heaviest in Europe.

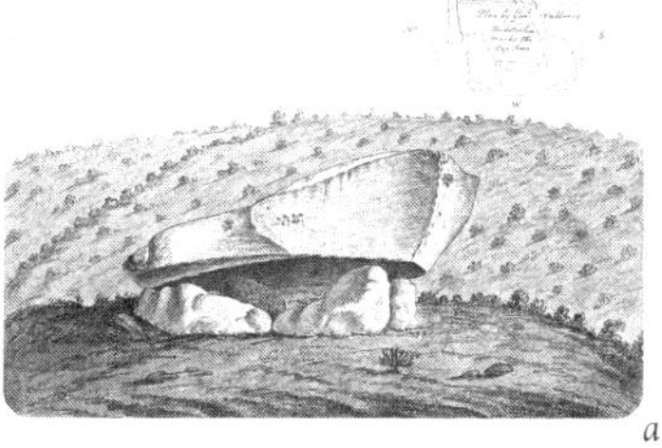

POULNABRONE & KILCLOONEY
dramatic architecture

POULNABRONE, CO. Clare. (*Poll na Brón*, 'Quernstone Hollow') is the second largest Irish portal tomb, with a 4×3m capstone, and 2m high orthostats (*see below*). The bones of twenty-one people were found here, with radiocarbon dates of c.3800–3200 BC. All had upper body arthritis from heavy labour; most had died before they were thirty, only one was over forty and two men had healed fractures, one to the skull, the other to a rib. The broken tip of a flint projectile was embedded in the hip bone of a third, which had not healed, so he must have died soon afterwards. The children's teeth showed bouts of illness and malnutrition, and many bones were scorched, suggesting a ritual purification. Along with these bones were those of many animals, as well as arrowheads, scrapers, stone disk beads and part of a bone pin. In the Bronze Age, c.1750–1420 BC, a newborn baby was buried near the entrance.

ABOVE: **KILCLOONEY**, co. Donegal (Cill Chluanadh Mhór, 'Church of the Large Meadow'). This portal tomb has a smaller version 9m behind it which was its mortuary chamber. It measures 2m long and 1.4m wide internally, and faces northeast. Two 1.8m high portal stones support the capstone which is 4.2m long and 3.7 m wide. A tall red granite stone makes the main back-stone, while all the others are grey granite. Pieces of a quartz-tempered pottery vessel of c.3780 to 3550 BC lay in the main chamber.

BELOW: Cairn Dolmen, Leanna, co. Clare, by William Frazer.

LINKARDSTOWN CISTS
to cap it all

The Linkardstown cists are part of a particular cultural development in a belt of land between counties Clare and Limerick and across to Dublin and Wicklow dating from c.3550–3350 BC. Each was covered by a substantial cairn, inside which was a slab-built cist topped with a large capstone. They contained up to three adults and occasionally children, and used a specific type of pottery: round-bottomed, shouldered pots decorated with geometric patterns.

KNOCKMAREE, co. Dublin, (*Cnoc Maraí*, Mariners' Hill). In 1838, labourers working under the employment of the Commissioners of Woods and Forests were ordered to dismantle a tumulus, 15 feet tall and 120 feet in circumference. In it they found four small stone cists (one shown below) in which were two crouched male skeletons aged about 40 to 50, a flint knife, a shell necklace, a bone toggle and a food vessel (below right).

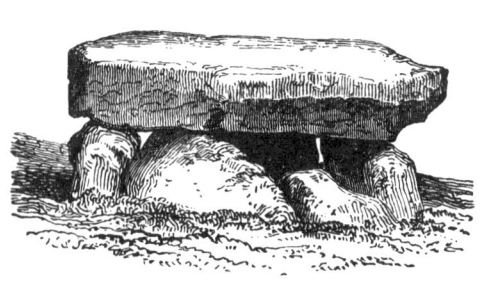

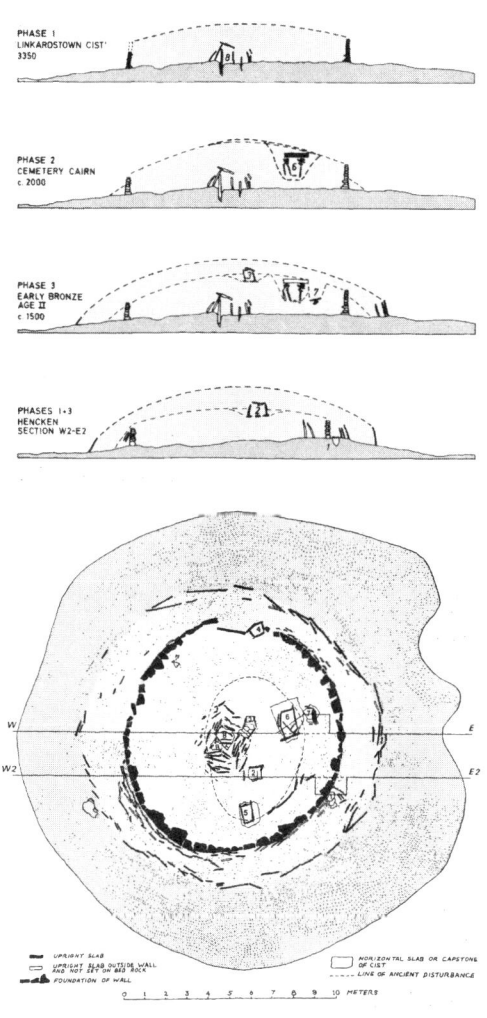

LEFT: **POULAWACK**, co. Clare (Poll a bhaic, 'Hole of the Bend') is only 2km from Poulnabrone portal tomb (see p.20). It has been carbon dated to c. 3350 BC, similar to Poulnabrone. Both were in use for nearly 2000 years. Poulawack's cist has two compartments, one held the bones of a middle-aged man and woman along with a younger woman and an oyster shell. In the other were an infant's bones, a flint scraper, a wild boar's tusk and two potsherds. Around 2000 BC three more cists were inserted, one with the unburnt bones of an adolescent and a child, plus a pottery sherd, and the second with the bones of an adult and a child. The third had two compartments, one held the cremated bones of a young man and the unburnt bones of an adolescent and a small child, the other held a man's bones with a Beaker pottery sherd. Circa 1600 - 1400 BC a crouched body was laid on the mound and covered with slabs over which a metre's thickness of soil and stones was added, and the new outer edge was defined by a second stone kerb. Three more cists were inserted into this cairn, one for an infant, another for a cremated adult, with a flint scraper and a bone point, and the third for a young woman.

THE LOUGHCREW COMPLEX
Co. Westmeath

The *Loch Craobh*, 'Lake of Trees', complex of tombs on the *Sliabh na Cailliagh* hills is spread over four hilltops, and dates from c.3300 BC.

Cairn T, the largest on Carnbane East is the Hag's Cairn or *Carn Bán*, ('the white cairn'). It has 38 kerbstones, most engraved, and was once covered in quartz pieces. The passageway leads to a 7m high cruciform chamber with three recesses, and a backstone with engraved solar symbols. The passage points 9° south of east, so the sun enters the chamber just after sunrise on both spring and autumn equinoxes.

The second largest, Cairn L, on Carnbane West, measures 40m across and has 41 kerb-stones. It has seven recesses formed with upright slabs. There are 18 decorated stones in the chamber, and at dawn on Samhain and Imbolc, the sun's rays light up the 2m limestone monolith outside the chamber's largest recess as well as its engraved back panel.

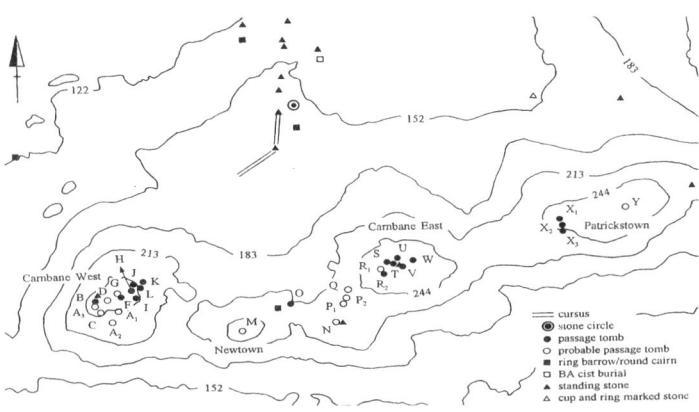

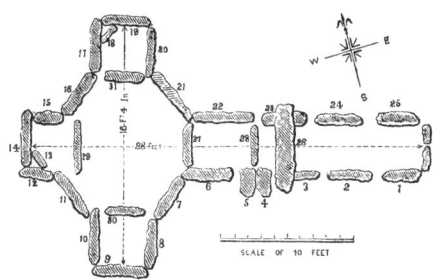
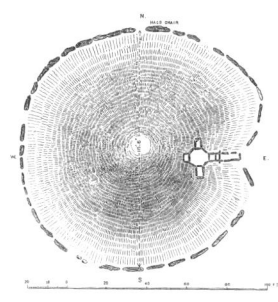

ABOVE LEFT: Plan of Loughcrew T.
ABOVE RIGHT: Loughcrew T showing kerbstones and cairn mound. LEFT: Cairn L before restoration, Martin 1895. BELOW LEFT: Stone basin and engraved panel in Cairn L. This panel is illuminated by the rising sun twice a year. BELOW RIGHT: The Keystone Stone in Cairn T. FACING PAGE: Map of the complex by Jean McMann.

THE BOYNE VALLEY COMPLEX
Dowth, Knowth and Newgrange

The *Brú na Bóinne* ('Mansion of the Boyne') is a complex of around 100 monuments nestled in a bend of the River Boyne in co. Meath (*see map below*). The site is dominated by the passage tombs of Newgrange (*p.28*), Knowth (*p.30*) and Dowth (*opposite*). They were built just after an ecological crisis c.3200 BC, which dimmed the sun and caused crop failures and famines for ten years. They contain the largest body of megalithic art in Europe, some of it astronomical.

Dowth (*Dubhadh*, 'Darkness') refers to the darkness broken by the king (*Bressal bó-dibad*) coupling with his sister at midwinter. When the mound was dug into in 1847 two partially collapsed passage tombs full of bones were found. Dowth North has a 14m passage, a 3m high cruciform chamber and is oriented towards Samhain and Imbolc sunsets while Dowth South's passage leads to a chamber with one recess, that is aligned towards winter solstice sunset.

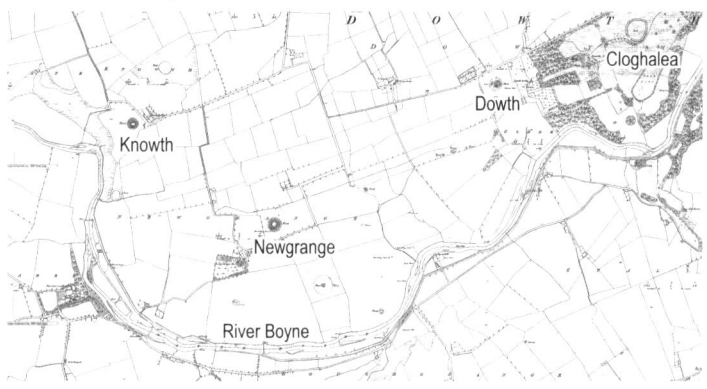

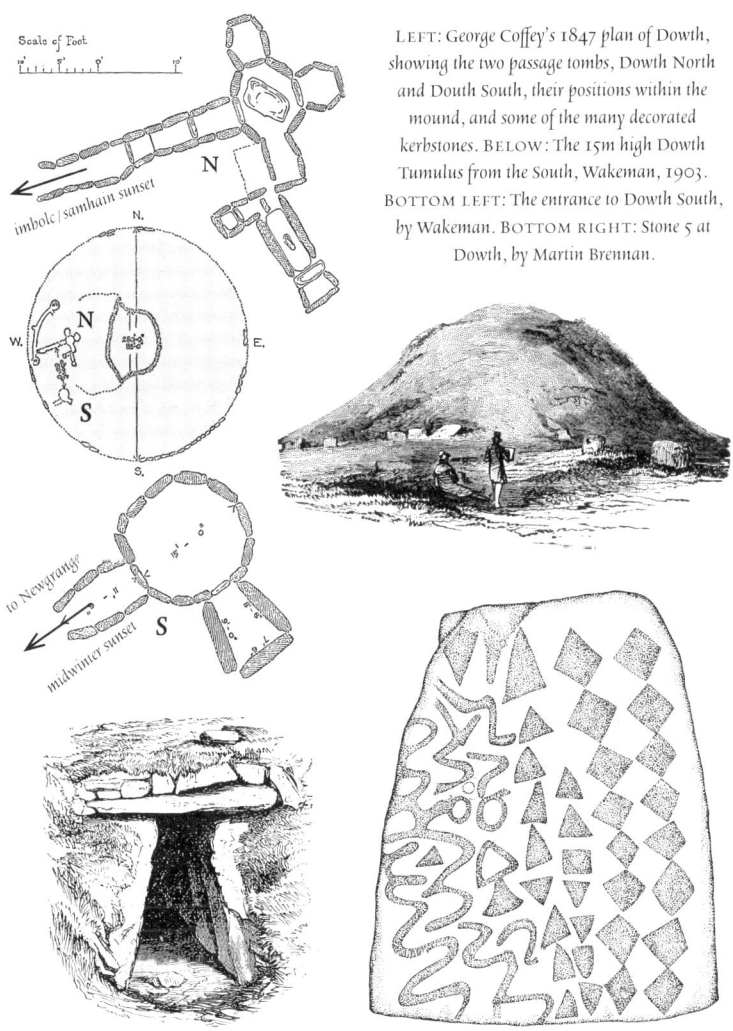

LEFT: George Coffey's 1847 plan of Dowth, showing the two passage tombs, Dowth North and Dowth South, their positions within the mound, and some of the many decorated kerbstones. BELOW: The 15m high Dowth Tumulus from the South, Wakeman, 1903. BOTTOM LEFT: The entrance to Dowth South, by Wakeman. BOTTOM RIGHT: Stone 5 at Dowth, by Martin Brennan.

NEWGRANGE
temple of the midwinter sun

The grandest of all passage tombs, Newgrange, or *Brú na Bóinne*, 'Bóinn's Feasting Hall', is 13m tall and was built c.3200BC. Its 18.9m passage leads to a 6m high cruciform chamber, off which lie three small chambers. The stonework is covered by large mound of alternating layers of earth and stone, edged by decorated kerbstones. 12 large stones form a segment of a circle around the entrance side of the tomb.

Many of the stones used in Brú na Bóinne were carried or dragged there from distant sources: gabbro pebbles from the Cooley Mountains, greywacke slabs from Clogherhead, granodiorite cobbles from the Mournes, and quartz from the Wicklow Hills.

Near the entrance, a stone-lined hollow cradled a symbolic stone phallus, hinting at the site's deep-rooted connection to fertility and creation beliefs. The structure was ingeniously aligned so that the sun's light pierced through the 'roof-box' during the midwinter solstice sunrise, but only if two quartz blocks were first removed from it. This phenomenon was intertwined with ancient Irish mythology, where the sun god Dagda is said to have united with the goddess Bóinn.

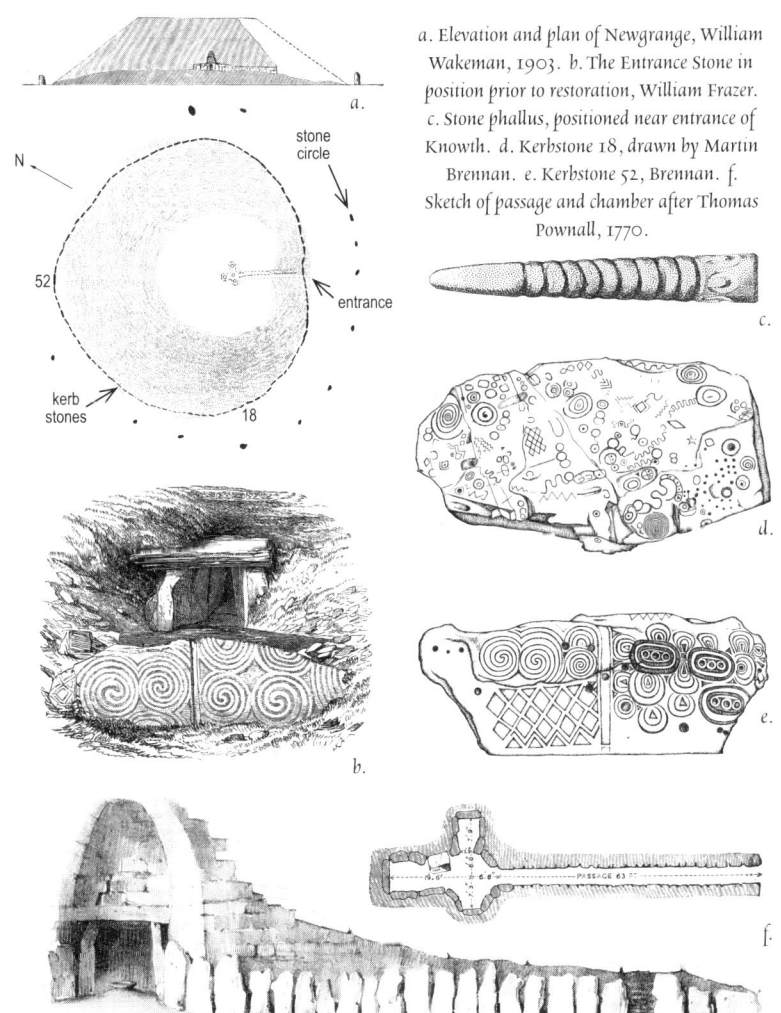

a. Elevation and plan of Newgrange, William Wakeman, 1903. b. The Entrance Stone in position prior to restoration, William Frazer. c. Stone phallus, positioned near entrance of Knowth. d. Kerbstone 18, drawn by Martin Brennan. e. Kerbstone 52, Brennan. f. Sketch of passage and chamber after Thomas Pownall, 1770.

KNOWTH
Cnóbha, Cnoc Buí, 'Hill of Buí'

Ireland's largest megalithic structure (12m high × 67m wide), Knowth, has 17 satellite tombs. Created c. 3200 BC, its two passages point east and west, with the eastern passage leading to Ireland's largest cruciform chamber (7m tall). Its backstone has an image carved on it which one researcher suggested may represent the full moon's mariae rotating as it traverses the sky. There are possible lunar representations on several more of Knowth's 400 carved stones, including on a large granite basin in the northern recess of its eastern chamber, near which a superb carved flint mace head was buried. (*below, top right*).

The eastern passage points 7° north of due east, allowing some light from the full moon to enter as well as sunrises near the equinox. The western passage lets in sunsets for twelve days before and after the equinoxes. Both passages have entrance stones with central vertical lines. A tall stone outside the western one casts its shadow over this line at equinox sunset. Quartz was originally spread over the mound and stone-lined hollows are found outside both entrances as well as a wood circle near the eastern one of c.2800–2500 BC.

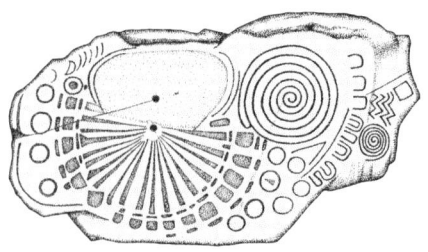

LEFT: Plan survey of Knowth, showing the 17 smaller satellite tombs, after Neil Carlin. BELOW: View of Knowth, showing some of the carved kerbstones at the site, by Martin Brennan. An arrow, left, points to the polar north. BOTTOM: Kerbstone 52 complex rows of designs were engraved over a large spiral and may record lunar cycles. FACING PAGE: Kerbstone 15 and flint mace from Knowth.

THE HILL OF TARA
and many cursuses

The Hill of Tara, near Skryne in co. Meath, is another important ceremonial site. It consists of numerous monuments and earthworks dating from the Neolithic to the Iron Age, including a passage tomb (the 'Mound of the Hostages', *below*), burial mounds, round enclosures, a standing stone (the 1m *Lia Fáil*, 'Stone of Destiny', *p.xx*) and a cursus.

Cursuses were major Neolithic monuments with parallel earthen banks and ditches, and the Irish examples are all associated with megalithic structures. Most are between 200m and 400m long, while the distance between the earthworks can be up to 90m. Often an enclosing bank runs between the earthworks at one or both ends.

They were constructed c.3400–3000 BC at several major Neolithic sites, while many more, particularly in Leinster, run up steep mountains to megalithic tombs near their summits. Several are oriented so the rising sun shines down them at the summer solstice or equinox, perhaps to make solar pathways for departing souls.

Tara's impressive cursus is about 200m long and has high parallel banks on either side of what was probably a processional way to the summit of the hill, which is covered with Neolithic monuments.

In the Middle Ages it was mistakenly identified as a banquetting hall ('*Teach Miodhchuarta*').

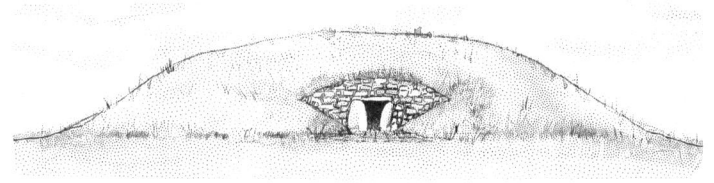

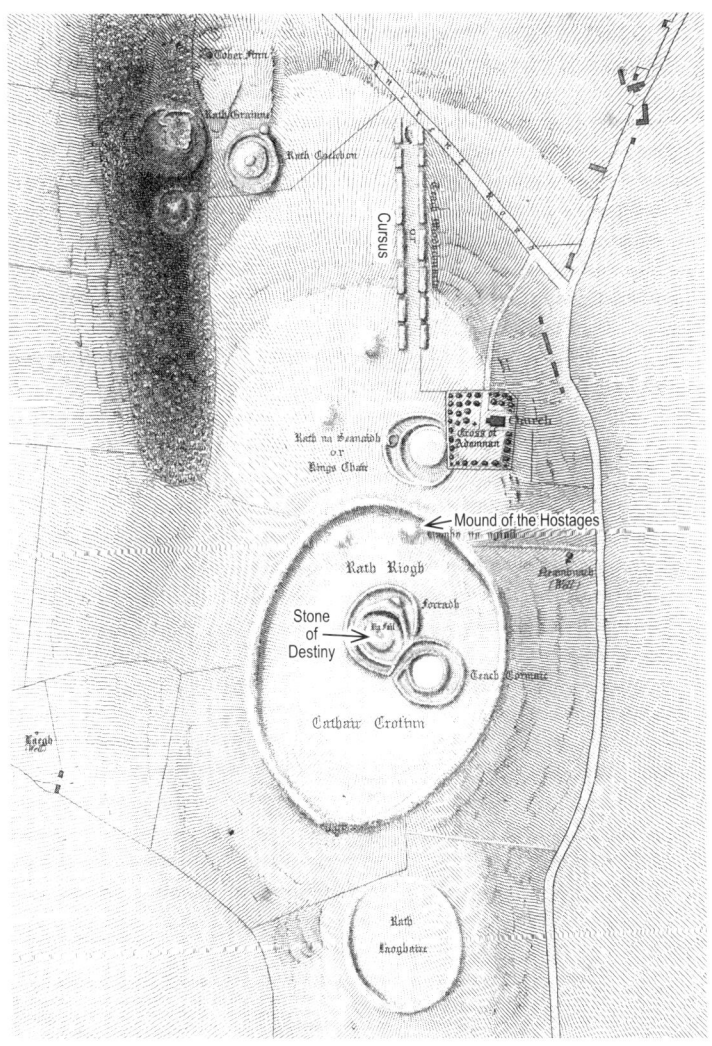

HENGES
circular banks and ditches

After 3200 BC, possibly in response to the decade of enfeebled sunlight, numerous henges—circular structures with stone or wooden uprights, earth banks and solar orientations—were constructed all over the British Isles. The first were at Orkney and Stonehenge, but they were soon in Ireland too, over 50 of them.

Several henges were created around *Brú na Bóinne*. Just east of Dowth c.3000 BC was built a 150m oval henge, Cloghalea (*Cloch liath*, 'Grey Stone'), with a 5m high bank with openings to midsummer sunrise and midwinter sunset (*lower opposite*). Another 200m henge lies to the south of Newgrange.

Other circular structures appeared around the same time. The twelve massive stones round Newgrange's southern half would have been part of a 104m circle, if completed, while two wooden circles near its entrance are dated to c.3018–2788 BC. There was also a c.2800–2500 BC wooden circle near the east entrance of Knowth, with many Orkney-style 'grooved-ware' pottery pieces being found here, as they have also been found around the henges. Some 150 small boulder circles were also built in the Sperrin Mountains c.2900–2600 BC. Other stone circles would later follow, mostly in the far north and south of Ireland.

Pollen and tree-ring analysis show that another major ecological upset affecting sunlight and plant growth for a decade occurred c.2345 BC. The probable cause was a large eruption of Hekla on Iceland. To make things worse, the bubonic plague also arrived. Ireland's ancient tales describing early populations killed off by famines, plagues and wars may well retain memories of such disasters.

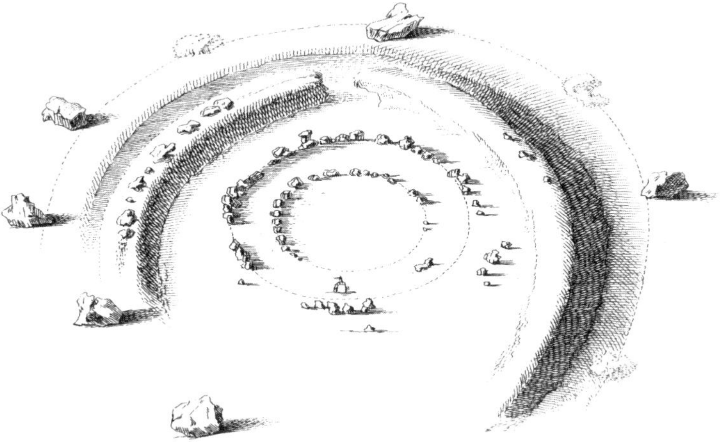

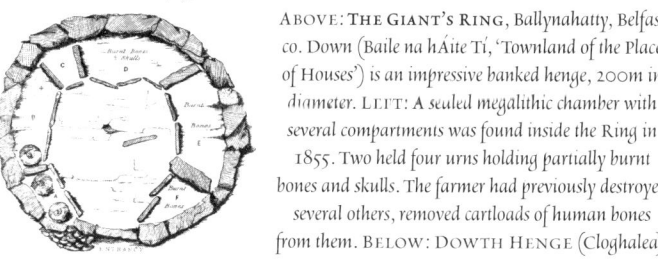

ABOVE: **THE GIANT'S RING**, Ballynahatty, Belfast co. Down (Baile na hÁite Tí, 'Townland of the Place of Houses') *is an impressive banked henge, 200m in diameter.* LEFT: *A sealed megalithic chamber with several compartments was found inside the Ring in 1855. Two held four urns holding partially burnt bones and skulls. The farmer had previously destroyed several others, removed cartloads of human bones from them.* BELOW: DOWTH HENGE (Cloghalea).

Grange & Ballynoe
two of the finest

THE GRANGE, co. Limerick, (*Líos*, 'Court') is the largest stone circle in Ireland, c.150m across, and dates from c.3000 BC (*opposite top*) Its twelve stones are integrated into the inner edge of a banked henge, and excavation found a litter of Neolithic and Beaker pottery on its old surface. A hole at its centre was probably for a post from which the circumference was measured. Each stone stands opposite one on the other side, and the two entrance portals are matched by two slabs on the southwest side whose sloping tops make a v-shape.

BALLYNOE (*Baile Nua* 'New Townland'), co. Down, is perhaps the finest Irish open stone circle. Two stones outside its western edge make a portal for its entrance, and opposite, on its eastern edge, is a quartz-rich stone, marking an alignment to equinox sunset. At 35m across, it resembles the Swinside and Castlerigg circles in Cumbria. In the Bronze Age an oval mound with heavy kerbstones was raised inside the circle with several burial cists, and a crescent of standing stones was raised outside the oval.

ABOVE: **GRANGE** stone circle and henge. Its most likely alignments are for Samhain sunset and midsummer sunrise. Concentric circles and arcs are carved on a stone north of the entrance. The largest stone, 4m tall and weighing over 50 tons, is at the NNE, possibly marking the northernmost moonrise. BELOW: **BALLYNOE** stone circle has over 50 stones. Illustrations by the author.

MORE STONE CIRCLES
they're still standing

There are around 250 stone circles in Ireland, most concentrated in the north and southwest of the island. The BELTANY STONE CIRCLE (Bealtaine, 'bright fire' or 'May Day'), co. Donegal, dates from the Bronze Age, and has sixty-four kerb stones enclosing an earth platform (*opposite top*). The tallest WSW stone faces a cup-marked triangular slab at the ENE making an alignment for May Day sunrise.

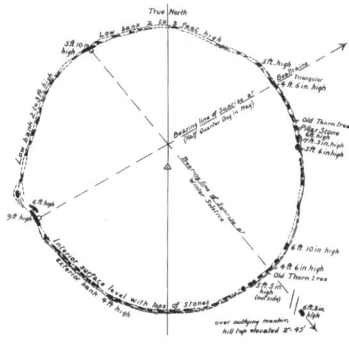

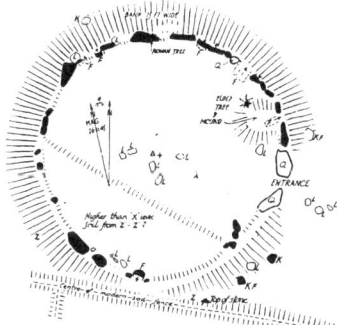

TOP LEFT: **Beltany** circle. TOP RIGHT: Distribution of stone circles (after Matthew Stout). LEFT: **Castleruddery** stone circle, co. Wicklow (Caislean an Ridire, the 'Castle of the Knights'), has twenty-nine stones, some decorated with cup marks. BELOW: **Summerbank** circle, Oldcastle, Co Meath - William Frazer. FACING PAGE: TOP: Four stone circles at **Cong**, drawn by Edward Lhuyd in 1699. BOTTOM: Double circle at Streedagh, 1880, by William Wakeman.

RECUMBENT STONE CIRCLES
shrines of the metal workers

Recumbent stone circles have a single large recumbent stone lying on its side, wedged between two upright standing stones (orthostats). They are found in north-east Scotland (where around 80 remain today) and south-west Ireland (co. Cork and co. Kerry), and date from the transitional period between the late Neolithic and the Early Bronze Age, c.2500–2000 BC. The recumbent stone is generally aligned with the moon's southernmost arc, which occurs once every eighteen and a half years, or towards the setting midwinter sun. Some examples are shown (*opposite*).

Over eighty stone rows were also erected at this time, pointing to the southwest. Excavations have found pits in the circles' interiors filled with charcoal, broken pottery and cremated human bones. Crushed quartz was also scattered near the recumbents, possibly drawing in the moon's power, or helping to rekindle the sun.

At DROMBEG, co. Cork, (*Droim Beag* 'Small Hill'), the site was carefully levelled c.1100 BC before the 9.3m circle was erected. The surviving thirteen stones are of local sandstone (*right*). Its 1.8m high portal stones face the recumbent stone on the SW side, indicating an orientation to midwinter sunset.

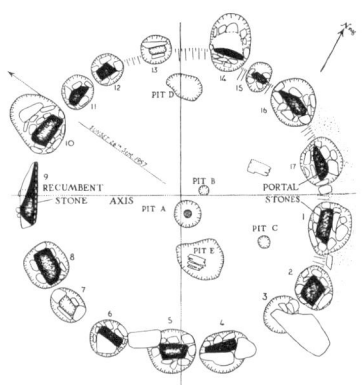

ABOVE: **TEMPLEBRYAN**, co. Cork (Teampall Bhriain 'Brian's Church'), has four upright stones, a fifth half fallen, and a quartz stone known as Cloch na Gréine, 'stone of the sun'. The recumbent stone has two horizontal veins of quartz running through it and another on its upper surface.

ABOVE: **KEALKILL**, co. Cork. (Caol Cill, 'Narrow Church'), one of the smallest rings in the British Isles, consists of five orthostats and a small recumbent stone. Excavated traces were found of two horizontal 2m long beams crossing each other in the centre of the ring, presumably to support a tall upright beam, 'like an American-Indian totem-pole'.

ABOVE & FACING PAGE: **DROMBEG**. The 1.9m wide recumbent stone has two cup marks, one with a ring around it, and the pecked outline of an axe. An engraving of an erect phallus on the inner side of the southern portal stone marks an alignment to the summer solstice sunrise, while a carving on the upper surface of the recumbent stone could be a vulva.

WEDGE TOMBS
double walled innovation

New megalithic monuments called wedge tombs arose in southwest Ireland at the same time as the recumbent stone circles, these were also oriented at the setting midwinter sun. They have double-walled rectangular or U-shaped chambers with substantial capstones, decreasing in height towards their east ends, while their west-facing entrances often had portals and porticos. About four hundred wedge tombs were erected c.2400–2100 BC.

KNOCKCURRAGHBOLA, CO. Tipperary (*Cnoc Corrbhuaile* 'Crab Apple Hill'), this impressive wedge-tomb crowns a knoll. It survives to a length of over 11m, with surviving double-walls on the south side, but its façade is missing. A door-slab and two capstones are still in place.

MOYLISHA WEDGE TOMB, CO. Wicklow (*Labbanasighe*, *Labba na Sí* 'Bed of the Spirits'), was excavated in 1937, when some potsherds, cremated bone and two stone disks were found, as well as two halves of a sandstone mould for casting spearheads.

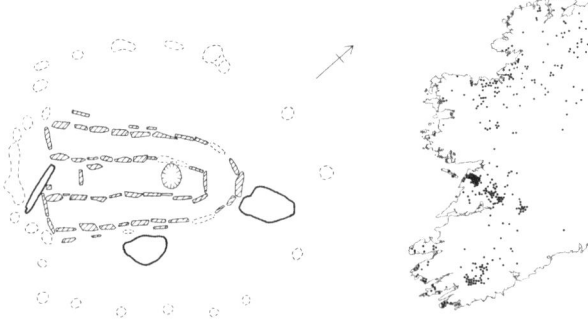

ABOVE and LEFT: **LOUGH GUR WEDGE TOMB**, CO. Tipperary (Loch Goir, 'Goir's Lake') was covered by a mound of stones until the 19th century. When excavated in 1938, fragments of cremated bone were found in a cist under the portico and the main chamber contained the unburnt bones of at least eight adults and several children as well as cattle and pig bones, Neolithic and Beaker pottery and some flints. Fragments of a crucible for melting metal were found near the portico, and part of a mould for casting a spear head. Radiocarbon dating indicates that it was in use c. 2500 to 2000 BC.

FACING PAGE: LEFT: Distribution of Wedge Tombs. RIGHT: **ISLAND WEDGE TOMB**, co. Cork, was created c. 2400 - 2000 BC by erecting the usual double row of orthostats in a 'U' shape with small stones packed between them, and flag capstones laid on top. Three deposits of cremated remains were found in covered hollows inside the tomb, each with a flint tool.

Labbacallee Wedge tomb
a murder mystery

LABBACALLEE, co. Cork (*Leaba Cailli* 'The Hag's Bed'), is the largest Irish wedge tomb, about 10m long by 6m wide. Uniquely, the tomb's east exterior has a formal facade of upright slabs.

Excavation found a partially decomposed reassembled woman's headless body, which had been left in a foetal position in a compartment in the tomb's eastern interior. This had then been filled with pottery pieces, animal bones, stones, earth, ash and cremated human bones before being sealed. Her skull was set between two pieces of a young man's broken skull in the main chamber, where his other remains and those of a five-year-old child and a newborn baby were put beside a thin upright slab, along with animal bones and fine pottery sherds. Crude pottery was left on its other side, and an opening was broken through the slab, sealing the compartment with the woman's body. Radiocarbon dating suggests this happened c.2200–2140BC.

Local legends say that this woman killed her husband, another that she rolled a boulder at him but missed, so the next day he rolled one at her and took her head clean off.

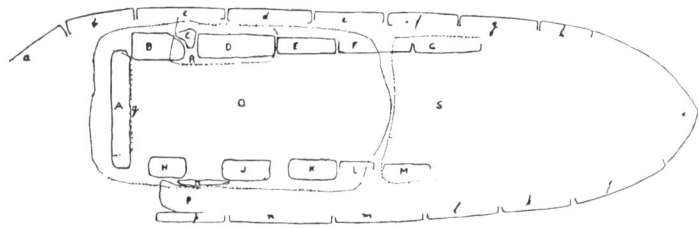

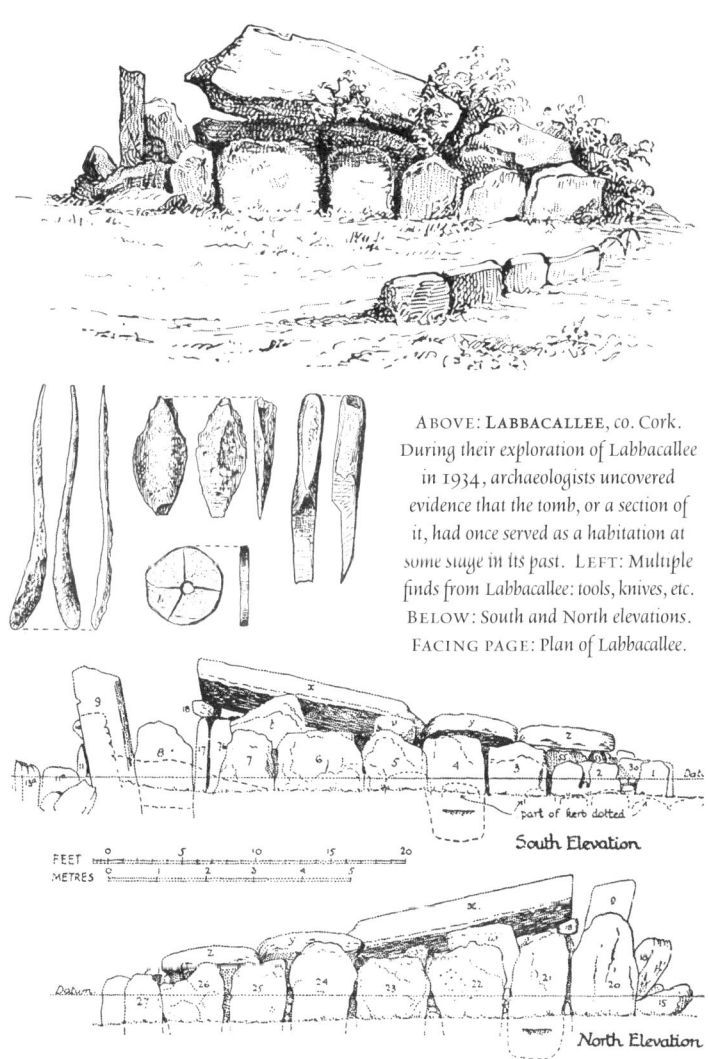

ABOVE: **LABBACALLEE**, co. Cork. During their exploration of Labbacallee in 1934, archaeologists uncovered evidence that the tomb, or a section of it, had once served as a habitation at some stage in its past. LEFT: Multiple finds from Labbacallee: tools, knives, etc. BELOW: South and North elevations. FACING PAGE: Plan of Labbacallee.

STONE ROWS
alignments to the heavens

Irish stone rows are mostly undated, but many are aligned towards winter solstice sunsets and are thought to be Bronze Age. Those associated with the cairns and stone circles in the Sperrin Mountains have been carbon dated to 2900–2600 BC and are aligned northeast, pointing to the most extreme northerly rising position of the moon.

BEAGHMORE (*Beitheach Mór*, 'Big Birchwood') consists of 7 circles, 10 stone rows and 12 carefully arranged cairns, at the foot of the Sperrin Mountains (*see plan below*). It was possibly an sacred astronomical site.

CASTLENALACHT, Bandon, co. Cork (*Caiseal na Lacht*, 'Castle of the Grave Mounds'). Four stones are aligned ENE over 13.5m.

BEENALAGHT, co Kerry (*Binn na Lacht*, 'Mountains of the Grave Mounds'). Five tall stones, oriented NE. One further stone is fallen.

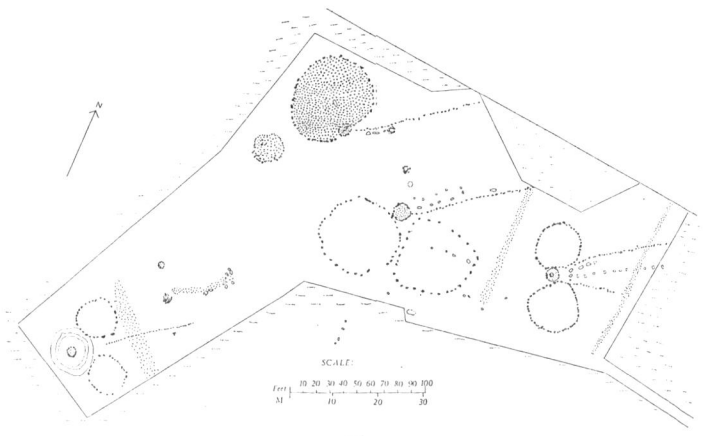

ABOVE: **EIGHTERCUA** stone row and megalithic tomb, Waterville, co. Kerry (Íochtair Cuan 'Lower Harbour'). c.1700BC. Four stones, the tallest 3m, are aligned E-W.

ABOVE: **GURRANES**, Castletownshend, co. Cork (Garrán, 'Grove'), also known as the 'Three Fingers'. Three tall slender stones, the highest being 4.3m high, are oriented on a NE-SW axis. Originally there were five stones; one was removed and the other is broken.

STANDING STONES
and epitaphs

There are countless Irish standing stones, mostly undatable. A few old Irish poems tell who is buried beneath particular named stones, so stories about them have long persisted.

THE LONG STONE, Punchestown, co. Kildare, is the tallest standing stone in Ireland, standing at 5.5m tall (*illustrated below*); it has another 1.5m buried in the ground. It toppled over in 1933 and was re-erected the following year, when a small cist tomb was also found nearby. Legend relates that Fionn MacCumhall threw the stone to its present location from Allen hill.

FORENAUGHTS, co. Kildare. (*Fornocht*, 'Naked'), also known as the 'Longstone Rath', has a henge bank forming a rough circle approx 50 to 60m in diameter with entrances facing east and west and a huge central granite standing stone, over 5m high and 0.75m wide. The interior rises slightly around the standing stone. A cist beside it had the burnt remains of an adult man and woman, pottery shards, beads and an archer's stone wrist guard. A vast fire had been burnt in the henge before the remains were put in the cist and the stone raised.

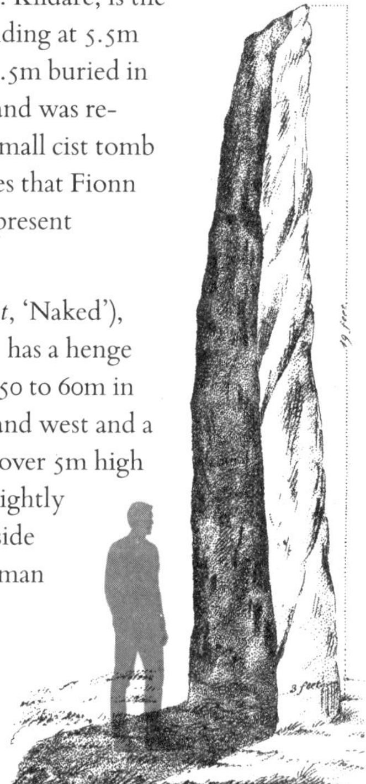

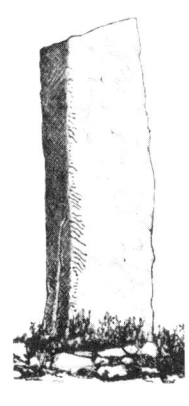 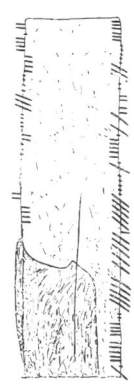

LEFT: **BREASTAGH** standing stone with ogham inscription, co, Mayo (Bréisteach, 'Rocky Place'). This superb square sectioned standing stone is 3.5 m high. It was probably erected in the Bronze Age, and has an ogham inscription which reads 'MAQ CORBBRI MAQ AMLONG[I]TT' 'Son of Corbbri, Son of Amlongitt'. Uniquely, it may record identifiable people as a Connacht king, Amlongaid, (d. c.440 – 450 CE) had a son called Coirpre.

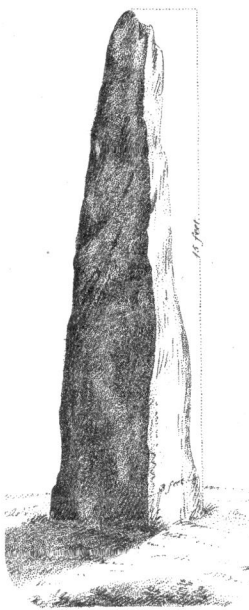  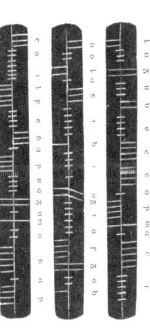

ABOVE: Holed stone at **OBERNAVEAN** in Woodville, Wakeman. RIGHT: Inscription on an Ogham stone the translation of which reads "Lugud, who died a lord or chieftain / On a day he was fishing / Is buried here in the grave's sanctuary". In this megalithic tradition, persisting until the time of the Roman occupation of Britain, some old standing stones were inscribed with ogham inscriptions, each giving the name of an individual or family. LEFT: The **CRADDOCKSTOWN LONGSTONE**, co. Kildare, is 4m tall and has developed a pronounced lean since this drawing.

MORE STANDING STONES
standing proud

Holed stones are found all over Ireland. They were believed to have the power to heal. For example, sickly children were passed through the large hole at the top of the stone *Cloch an Phoill* ("Stone of the Hole") in the townland of Aghade, near Tullow, Co.

The HOLE STONE, Doagh, co. Antrim, (*Dumhach*, 'Mound') stands on a rocky outcrop in a field and it is used as a "love stone," for commemorating betrothals (*below left*). The hole is only big enough for a woman's hand, so her lover has to hold hers on the other side. It is said that a man who broke the vows made here on that night was cursed to roam as a black horse for eternity.

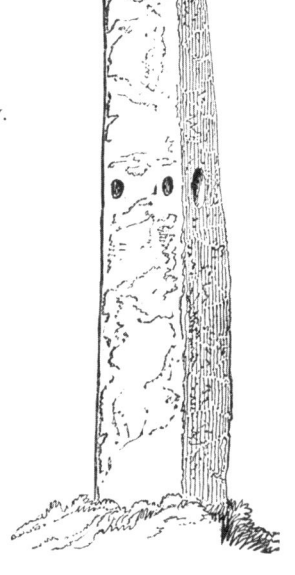

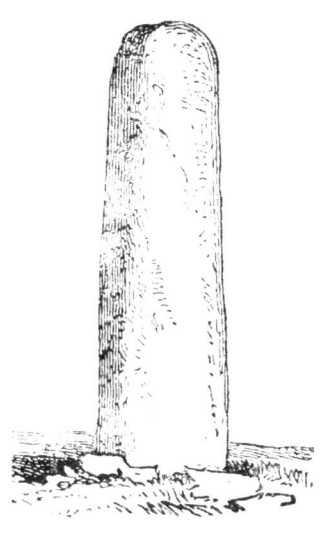

LEFT: **LIA FÁIL**, Tara, co. Meath. The 'Stone of Destiny' or 'Speaking Stone' is said to have been the inauguration stone for Ireland's High Kings. (see too p.xx). It was supposedly brought to Ireland by the Tuatha Dé Danann, from the "Northern Isles". It would roar with rage at a false king, or with joy for a rightful one, to whom it would give power and a long life. Cúchulainn split it with his sword when it did not cry out for his protégé, after which it was silent until it hailed Conn of the Hundred Battles and then Brian Ború.

BELOW LEFT: **THE CAT STONE**, (Aill na Mireann, 'Stone of Divisions'), Uisneach, co. Westmeath. This large stone on the side of the Hill of Uisneach was held to be the exact centre of Ireland, and that the division lines of the four provinces meet here. It looks like a squatting cat.

FACING PAGE LEFT: The **HOLE STONE**, Doagh, co. Antrim. FACING PAGE RIGHT: **HOLED STONE** at the 'Church of the Men', Inismurray, co. Sligo, W. F. Wakeman, 1909. ABOVE RIGHT: **Standing Stone of COAD** near Corofin, co. Clare, by Wakeman.

MYSTICAL MEMORIES
visions of heaven and hell

Numerous Irish stories exist about megalithic sites, some of which may go back to the times of their use. Many megalithic sites were assigned to the druids, with names such as Druid's Altar (for Drombeg, *p.xx*) Druid's Stone and Druid's Chair (*both shown opposite*).

Remarkably, an archaeologist in western Ireland found a community that has a yearly mass said for the souls of people in a local megalithic cemetery, and until the 1860s, people climbed SLIEVE DONARD on St John's day near the summer solstice, to hear a mass said in its passage tomb. It was said that at certain times one could be taken to Donard, one of seven men sent into mountains by St Patrick to watch over Ireland until the last day.

Another tale says St Patrick entered LOUGH DERG's pagan sanctuary, a passage tomb, to see hell (*centre of the island, right*). Many followed his example, fasting and praying without sleep for two weeks before being shut into it for a night and a day, to experience hallucinations, as people must have done since Neolithic times.

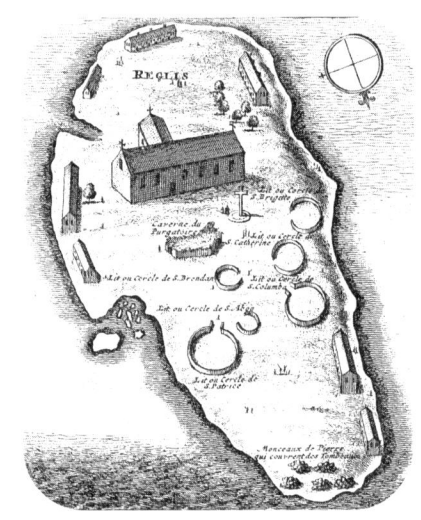

FACING PAGE: Map of Station Island, St Patrick's Purgatory, Lough Derg, co. Donegal, c.1707.

Memories of the Druids:
ABOVE: The Druid's Rocking Chair, Buloock, Dublin, Beranger 1776. LEFT: The Druids Judgement Seat, Dublin. BOTTOM: The Druid's Stone, Magheraboy, co Antrim. Julius Caesar famously wrote of the druids: "The Druids believe that their religion forbids them to commit their teachings to writing, although for most other purposes the Gaul's (Celts) use the Greek alphabet. But I imagine this rule was originally established for other reasons – because they did not want their doctrine to become public property, and in order to prevent their pupils from relying on the written word and neglecting to train their memories."

STONE MAGIC
bulláuns and transformations

This short tour of Ireland's megalithic wonders now comes to an end. So what have we learnt? The people who erected these monumental structures must have been driven by profound purposes, to skillfully transport and balance such stones at their carefully selected sites.

Intriguingly, the intricate carvings on numerous stones resemble the entoptic patterns perceived during altered states of consciousness. Perhaps Neolithic people sought sensory deprivation within dark chambers to induce visionary experiences, and afterwards carved these 'magical visions' onto their monuments' stones.

Some traditions persist even today, like the ritual of rotating smooth stones nestled in *bulláuns*, natural or man-made depressions in rock surfaces to invoke blessings or cast spells (*shown opposite*).

The enduring enchantment of these old stones is vividly illustrated in the lore surrounding the Lissyviggeen stone circle, also known as 'The Seven Sisters', a name which pays homage to the daughters of Ernmas, a revered figure in Irish mythology. According to the legend, on Beltane, it was forbidden to commence festivities before dawn. Yet, on one such occasion, a druid stumbled upon seven children joyously dancing under the moonlight, watched over by their beaming parents. In response, he transformed them into stone. Miraculously, on the eve of every May, they are said to briefly reclaim their human forms, dancing jubilantly under the midnight sky.

LEFT: The 'cursing stones' at Killinagh, Co Cavan, drawn by Wakeman in 1875. Superstitions still persist about these bulláuns, which are often linked to revered springs or wells, though their original meanings are now mostly obscure.

ABOVE LEFT: Bulláun near Tyredagh Castle, Tulla, co. Clare, by William Frazer. RIGHT: Gortaloughan, Bulláun Stone, by Wakeman, 1875. BELOW: An Ancient Irish Repast, by Henry Beauford c.1790, connects the Neolithic, druidic and everyday worlds.

IRELAND'S MAIN MEGALITHIC SITES

AGHANAGLACK, co. Fermanagh, (*Achadh na Glaice*, 'Field of the Hollow'), court cairn.

ANNAGHMARE, co. Armagh (*Áth na Marbh*, 'Ford of the Dead'), court cairn.

ANTYNANUM, co. Antrim (*An Tigh nAnam* 'The House of Souls'), court cairns.

ATHGREANY, co. Wicklow (*Achadh Gréine*, 'Field of the Sun'), stone circle.

AUDLEYSTOWN, co. Down is a dual-court tomb.

ANNAGHMARE, co. Armagh (*Áth na Marbh*, 'Ford of the Dead'), court cairn.

BALLYGLASS, co. Mayo, (*Baile Glas*, 'Grey Townland'), court cairn.

BALLYKEEL DOLMEN, co. Armagh, (*Baile Caol*, 'Narrow Townland'), portal tomb.

BALLYMACALDRACK (Dooey's Cairn), co. Antrim (*Baile Mhic Ualdraig*, 'MacAldrack's Townland'), court cairn.

BALLYMACDERMOT, co. Armagh ('MacDermot's Townland'), court cairn.

BALLYNOE, co. Down. (*Baile Nua* 'New Townland'), stone circle.

BEAGHMORE, co. Tyrone (*Bheitheach Mhór*, 'Big Birchwood'), henge and stone rows.

BEENALAGHT, co Kerry (*Binn na Lacht*, 'Mountains of the Grave Mounds'), stone row.

BELTANY, co. Donegal. (*Bealtaine*, 'MayDay'), stone circle.

BREASTAGH, co. Mayo (*Bréisteach*, 'Rocky Place'), standing stone with ogham inscription.

BROWNSHILL DOLMEN, co. Carlow (*Dolmain Chnoic an Bhrúnaigh*), portal tomb.

BRÚ NA BÓINNE Complex, co. Meath ('*Bóinn's* Feasting Hall').

CARRICKGLASS DOLMEN, co. Sligo (*Carraig Glás*, 'Grey Rock'), portal tomb.

CARROWKEEL complex, co. Sligo (*Ceathrú Caol*, 'Narrow Quarterland'), passage tomb.

CARROWMORE, co. Sligo (*Ceathrú Mór*, 'Big Quarterland') , megalithic cemetery.

CASHELKEELTY, co. Kerry, on the Béarra Peninsula. recumbent stone circle.

CASTLENALACHT, Bandon, co. Cork (*Caiseal na Lacht*, 'Castle of the Grave Mounds'), stone row.

CASTLERUDDERY, co. Wicklow (*Caislean an Ridíre*, the 'Castle of the Knights'), stone circle.

THE CAT STONE, Uisneach, co. Westmeath (*Aill na Mireann*, 'Stone of Divisions'), standing stone.

CLOCHAFARMORE, co. Louth, (*Cloch an Fir Mhóir*, 'Stone of the Big Man'), standing stone.

CLOGHALEA, Nr Dowth (*Cloch liath*, 'Grey Stone'), oval henge.

CLONTYGORA, co. Armagh (*Cluainte gabhra*, 'Goats' Meadows'), court cairn.

COHAW, co. Cavan (*Cothabháil* 'Sustenance'), court cairn.

CREEVYKEEL, co. Sligo, (*Chraobhach Caol* 'Narrow Thicket'), court cairn.

DOWTH, co. Meath (*Dubhadh*, 'Darkness'), large megalithic site.

DROMBEG, co. Cork, (*Droim Beag* 'Small Hill'), recumbent stone circle.

DROMBOHILLY, co. Kerry. (*Droim Buachalla* 'Boy's Hill'), recumbent stone circle.

EIGHTERCUA, Waterville, co. Kerry (*Íochtair Cuan* 'Lower Harbour'), stone row.

FARRANMACBRIDE, Columbkille Glen, co. Donegal (*Fearann Mhic Giolla Bhríde*, McGillbride's land, Gleann Cholm Cille), court cairn.

FOURKNOCKS, co. Meath (*Fuair Cnoic*, 'Cold Hills'), passage tomb.

FORENAUGHTS, co. Kildare. (*Fornocht*, 'Naked') aka 'Longstone Rath', standing stone.

GIANT'S RING, Ballynahatty, Belfast co. Down (*Baile na hÁite Tí*, 'Townland of the Place of Houses'), stone circles,

GRANGE, co. Limerick, (*Líos*, 'Court') the largest stone circle in Ireland.

GURRANES, Castletownshend, co. Cork (*Garrán*, 'Grove'), stone row.

HARRISTOWN DOLMEN on the eastern slopes of Brown Mountain, co. Kilkenny, portal tomb.

THE HOLE STONE, Doagh, co. Antrim, (*Dumhach*, 'Mound'), standing stone.

HOWTH DOLMEN, co. Dublin, or Aideen's Grave, is near Howth Castle, portal tomb.

ISLAND WEDGE TOMB, co. Cork.

KEADEEN CURSUS, co. Wicklow (*Chidden*, 'Flat-topped hill')

KEALKILL, co. Cork. (*Caol Cill*, 'Narrow Church'), recumbent stone circle.

KENMARE, co. Kerry (*Ceann Mhara* 'Sea Headland'), recumbent stone circle.

KILCLOONEY, co. Donegal (*Cill Chluanadh Mhór* 'Church of the Large Meadow'), portal tomb.

KILLACLOHANE, co. Kerry (*Coill an Chlocháin*, 'Church of the Strong Ford'), portal tomb.

KILMOGUE, co Kilkenny (*Cill Mhóg*, 'Mogue's church'), portal tomb.

THE KISSING STONE, co Silgo (*Leaba na Fian*, 'Warriors' Bed'), part of the Carrowmore Dolmen site, passage tomb.

KNOCKCURRAGHBOLA, co. Tipperary (*Cnoc Corrbhuaile* 'Crab Apple Hill'), wedge tomb.

KNOCKMANY, or Anya's Cove, co. Tyrone (*Cnoc mBáine*, 'Báine's Hill'), passage tomb.

KNOCKMAREE, co. Dublin. (*Cnoc Maraí*, Mariners' Hill), Linkardstown cist.

KNOCKROE, co. Kilkenny (*Cnoc Rua* 'Red Hil'), passage tomb.

KNOWTH, co. Meath (*Cnóbha, Cnoc Buí*, 'Hill of Buí'), passage tomb, timber circle or woodhenge.

LABBACALLEE, co. Cork, (*Leaba Cailli* 'The Hag's Bed'), wedge tomb.

THE LABBY ROCK, Carrickglass, co. Sligo (*Leaba*, 'Bed'), portal tomb.

LIA FÁIL, Tara co. Meath 'Stone of Destiny' or 'Speaking Stone', standing stone.

LISSYVIGGEEN, co. Kerry (*Lios Uí Bhigín* 'Uí Bhigín's Fort'), recumbent stone circle.

LISTOGHIL, co Sligo (*Lios a' tSeagail*, 'Rye Court'), court cairn situtated at Carrowmore.

LOUGH DERG, co. Donegal (*Loch Dearg*, 'Red Lake'), one of the oldest pilgrimage sites in Christendom.

LOUGHCREW complex, co. Westmeath (*Loch Craobh*, 'Lake of Trees'), home to the Hag's Cairn.

LOUGH GUR, co. Tipperary (*Loch Goir*, 'Goir's Lake'), wedge tomb.

MAGHERABOY, co Sligo (*Machaire Buí*, 'Yellow plain'), causewayed enclosure.

MAGHERAGHANRUSH, Deerpark, co. Sligo, (*Machaire Chon Rois*, 'the Plain of Ros's Hound'), court cairn.

MAUGHANSILLY, Kealkill co, Kerry (*Macha na Sailí* 'Pasture of the Willows'), stone row.

MILLIN BAY, co. Down (*Millín*, 'Small Mound'), passage tomb.

THE MOUND OF THE HOSTAGES, co. Meath (*Dumha na nGiall*), passage tomb.

MOYLISHA, co Wicklow (*Labbanasighe, Labba na Sí* 'Bed of the Spirits'), wedge tomb.

NEWGRANGE, co. Meath, (*Brú na Bóinne*, the 'Feasting Hall of Bóinn'), large megalithic site with passage tomb and henges.

OGHIL, co. Galway (*Eochaill*, 'Yew Wood'), wedge tomb.

PROLEEK DOLMEN, co. Louth (*Brú Leac*, the 'Bruised Stone'), passage tomb.

POULNABRONE, co. Clare. (*Poll na Brón*, 'Quernstone Hollow'), portal tomb.

POULAWACK, co. Clare (*Poll a bhaic*, 'Hole of the Bend') is only 2km from Poulnabrone portal tomb.

PUNCHESTOWN LONG STONE, co. Kildare, is a standing stone located just outside the racecourse.

RATHLACKEN, co. Mayo, (*Ráth Leacáin* 'Fort of Stone Slabs'), court cairn.

SEEFIN, co. Wicklow (*Suí Fionn*, 'Fionn's Seat'), passage tomb.

SHANBALLYEDMUND, co. Tipperary (*Seanbhaile Éamainn*, 'Éamann's old townland'), court cairn.

SLIEVE GULLION, co. Armagh (*Sliabh gCallann* 'Mountain of loud Storms'), passage tomb.

SLIEVENAMON, co. Kilkenny (*Sliabh na mBán*, 'Mountain of the Women'), cursus.

TINRYLAND, co. Carlow (*Teach an Raoilinn*, 'House of Raoilinn'), Linkardstown cists.

URAGH CIRCLE, co. Kerry, (*Iúbhrach*, 'Land of Yew Trees'), recumbent stone circle.

The author would like to thank the following for their assistance with this book:

Father Michael O'Flanagan's History & Heritage Centre (visit their excellent and exhaustive website www.carrowkeel.com if you want more detail about any of the sites mentioned in this book); Sligo Museum; The National Library of Ireland; The Digital Repository of Ireland; The Royal Irish Academy; Martin Brennan (do read his seminal book 'The Stars and the Stones'). Pictures have been taken from: William Wakeman's Handbook of Irish Antiquities, 1891 & Archæologia Hibernica, 1905; Borlase, Dolmens of Ireland, 1895; The Antiquities of Ireland by Francis Grose, 1791; and others.

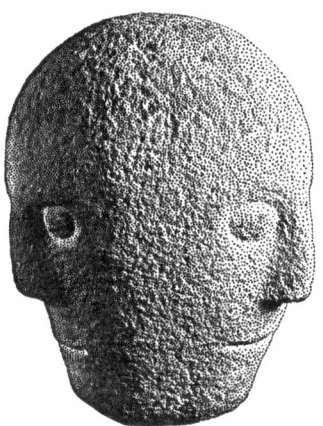

ABOVE: *The Corleck Head, a three-faced stone idol, 33cm high, was found in a 2500BC passage tomb, near Drumeague in 1855. It was found with the Corraghy head, a double-headed stone sculpture with a ram's head on one side and a bearded human's on the other.*